Master Prezi in 10 Easy Steps & Become a Better Presenter

THE ULTIMATE Prezi COURSE

SAID ARAR

The Ultimate Prezi Course

Master Prezi in 10 Easy Lessons

By

Said Arar

Become a Better Presenter

Making a presentation puts you on public display. Your audience will not only listen to your ideas, they will also respond to the way you present them. You will need more than a well written presentation to make an impact. You will need to deliver it in a flexible and interesting way, and the software you will use is crucial in such situation.

There is no doubt that Prezi is the best presentation software in the market. And this simple, step-by-step book, written in a down-to-earth and direct language is the ultimate way to learn this beautiful software.

Written by a Prezi expert with over 5 years of experience and mastery of the software. Who worked with world-class clients such as *Krauthammer*, *SerendiWorld*, *Changi Airport Group*, *Pitcher Partners* and many others.

There are two reasons behind writing this book. The first is that most of the other books about Prezi are out of date. Prezi is a fast-changing software, always being improved, so let's be honest, trying to learn Prezi from a book based on last year version will not help you much. This book is based on the last version to date.

The second reason is that most of the other books are theoretical with long reading chapters, with no illustrations or snapshots. Why would you read about the importance of mind-mapping and the history of PowerPoint if your reason behind buying a book is just to learn Prezi! This is a practical manual, we will guide you step by step through all Prezi features with illustrations, software snapshots and internet links, because the first step to create great Prezi presentations is to master all the software features.

My job is to help you create the best Prezi presentations by going through all Prezi features and options one by one.

Said

Email: arar.said@hotmail.com

Table of Contents

Introduction

About Prezi

Prezi is a virtual whiteboard that allows to the user to organize his ideas and his presentation content in a two dimensional plan in different and creative ways, since the user is not limited to the linear and traditional way of presenting using slides like in other software such as PowerPoint. Prezi gives more options to create awesome presentations that your audience will remember through its 2D plan and zooming features.

What we cover in this book

This is a practical manual, so we will take you step by step through all Prezi features, starting from how to insert texts and images in your presentation, concluding with more advanced tips on how to create a great prezi.

How to use this book

Since this is a practical guide, I recommend that you sit in front of a computer with Prezi being installed on it, in order to follow and practice all the steps that you'll find here.

What you will need

Once you create your Prezi account and sign up for the license that suits you, all you need is a computer and a cup of coffee.

Lesson I

Prezi Interface
&
Creating Prezi Presentations from Scratch

Prezi Interface

A Prezi presentation sits on a Canvas or a work space. Think of this space as a table where you can freely move your objects around. So in this sense, Prezi is much different than other traditional presentation software such as PowerPoint, as you are not limited to linear navigation between the slides.

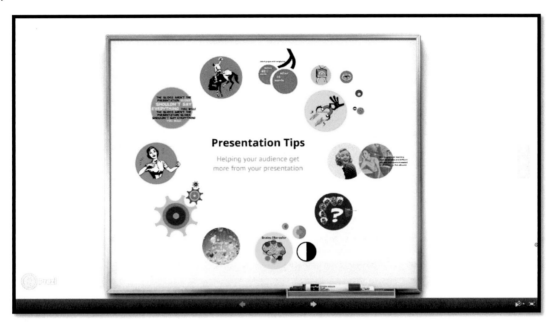

Creating Prezi Presentations from Scratch

To start a new prezi, you have two options:

1. You can start a new presentation from your Prezi.com personal account after opening one.

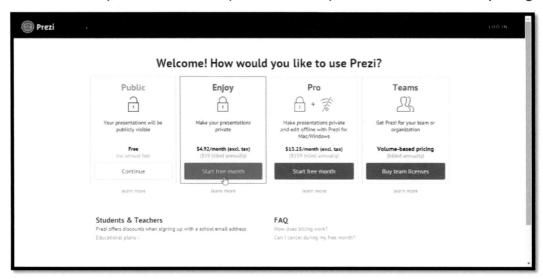

But keep in mind that all your presentations will be public if you open a Public Account.

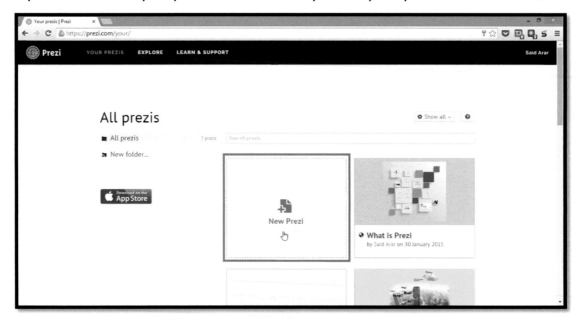

2. You can download the **Prezi Desktop Software** and in this case you can:

- Start a **New synced prezi** (which will be automatically synced with your Prezi.com account).

Or

- Start a **New local prezi** (which will be only on your computer until you decide to sync it yourself).

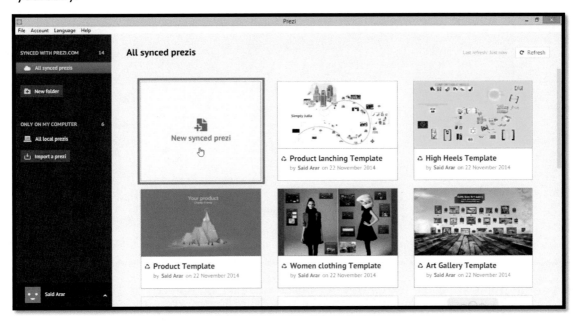

After starting a new prezi, you can either use the existing templates or start a blank prezi. We will explore templates later, let's start now with a blank prezi.

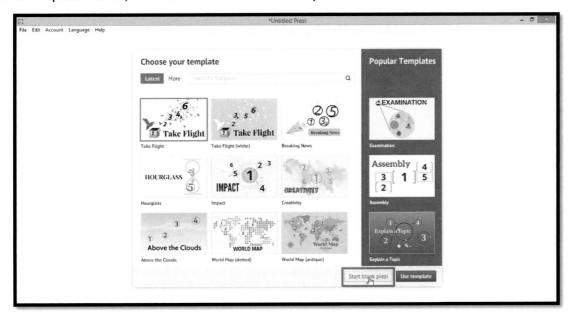

When you start a new presentation from scratch, you will see a blank canvas or work space with a single frame. Currently our frame is a circle; frames are similar to slides in PowerPoint.

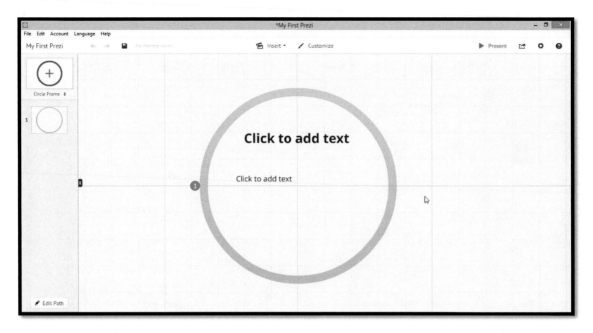

To insert additional frames, go to the top of the screen, click on **Insert**, then click on **Layouts...**

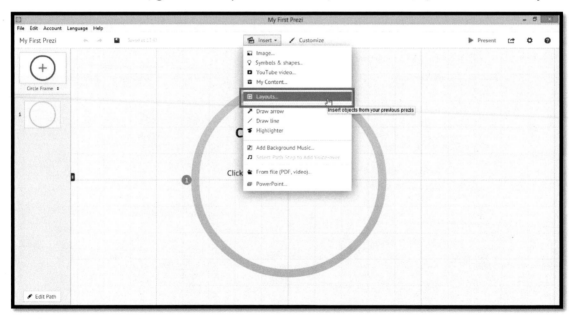

On the right side of the screen, you will see a list of **Single Frames** and another list of **Multi-Frames**. To add the frame that you like, either double-click on it; or click, hold and drag it to the canvas.

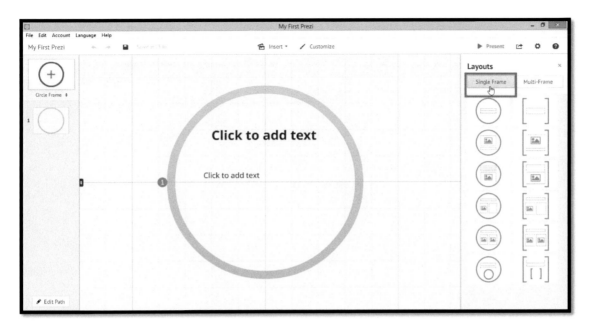

Again, think of these frames as your slides.

You can freely navigate your canvas, click and hold to go left or right, up or down, you can use your mouse wheel to zoom in or zoom out. On the right side of your screen you will see a **Home** button, a plus sign (**+**) and a minus sign (**-**). Use them to zoom in or zoom out. Click on the **Home** icon to show an overview of your canvas, this will fit entire objects to your screen.

You can double-click on any frame to zoom in.

If you want to quickly add a single frame, go to the top left of the screen and click on the frame icon.

You can also choose what type of frame you want to add. You have four different options: Bracket, Circle, Rectangle or Invisible. Select which type of frame you want to add, and then click on it to drag it to your canvas.

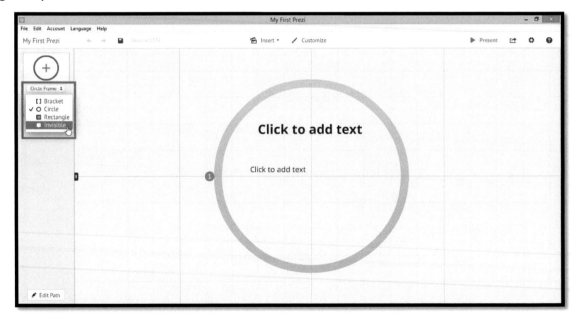

Let's now explore the **Menu** items located at the top bar. On the left you will see the **name** of your file, the **Undo**, **Redo** and **Save** buttons. Even though Prezi saves your work automatically every two minutes, you still can save your work manually by pressing on the **Save** button. In the middle of the top bar, you will see the **Insert** menu where you can add images, videos, etc...

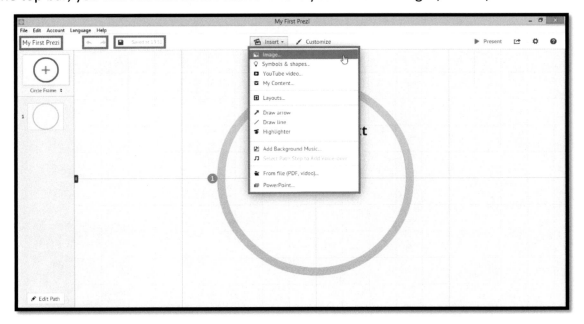

And you have the **Customize** button. This button will help you to add a background image for your prezi, choose a theme, or even customize a personal theme...

On the right of the top bar you will see the **Present**, **Share**, **Settings** and **Help** buttons. I would like to show you how to activate the keyboard shortcuts for your prezi. Click on the **Settings** menu, and enable shortcuts. You may click on the little question mark (**?**) to see the available shortcuts in Prezi.

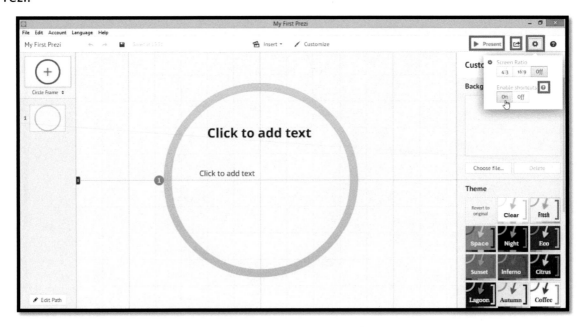

The following web page will open in your browser:

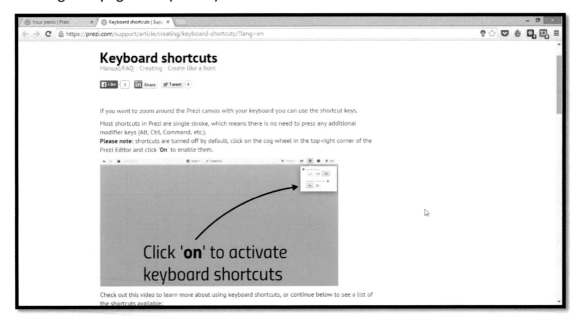

Some of the available shortcuts are frequently used such as: **CTRL+S** for saving; copying and pasting commands such as **CTRL+C** and **CTRL+V** can also being used in Prezi. Lastly, use your **Space** key to enter the **Present** mode and press again to exit that mode. Let's also explore some of the shortcuts for running your presentation. You may use **Left** and **Right** arrows of your keyboard to proceed back and forth in your presentation, or **Up** and **Down** arrows to zoom in and out. Also use your mouse wheel to zoom in and out. You may also play your presentation automatically by clicking on the button right below the presentation (Remember to open the **Present** mode first).

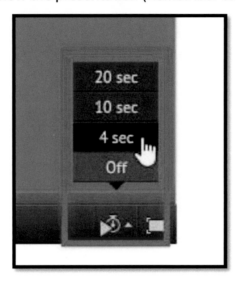

Currently you can set up your presentation to 4, 10 or 20 seconds as the duration to stay on each frame.

Lesson 2

Working with Texts & Images in Prezi

Inserting and Editing Texts

You can left click anywhere on the canvas to insert a text.

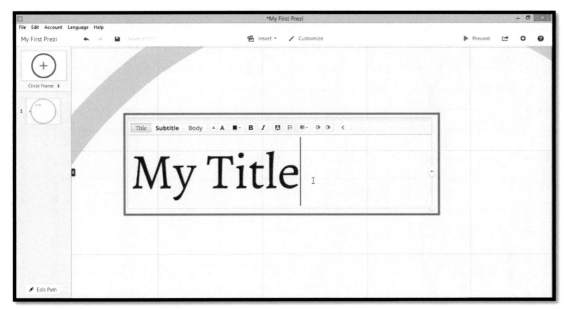

As you can see, you can easily convert your text to a Title.

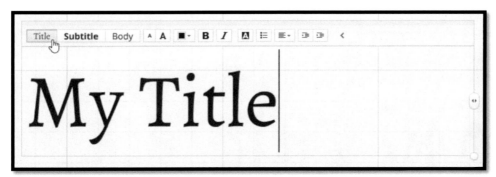

Or a Subtitle.

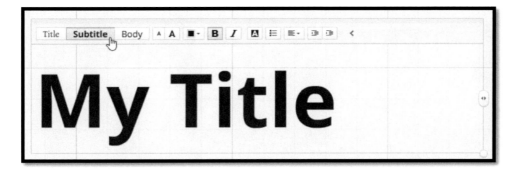

Or a Body text.

You can also increase or decrease the size of your text.

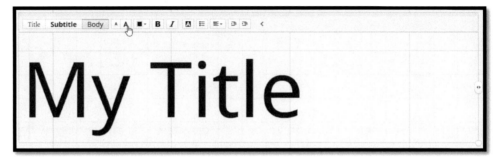

Change its color.

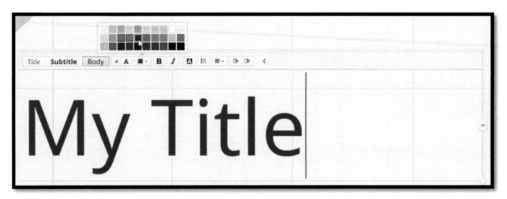

Make it **Bold**.

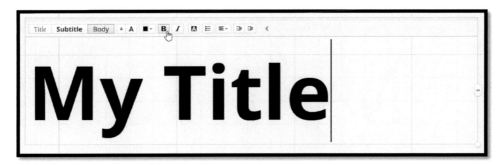

Or *Italic*.

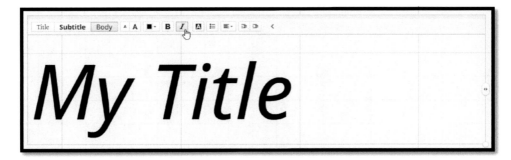

And put a background color (in this example it's the light grey color).

And you can add bullets.

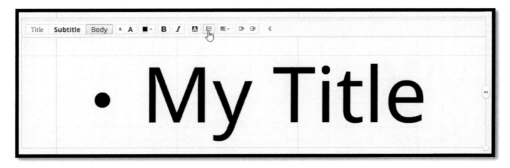

Or change the alignment options such as left aligned, right aligned, center aligned or justified.

And you can change the indenting of your text.

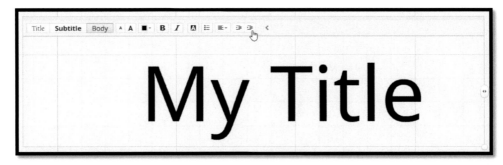

Every time you want to further edit a text item, click on this text item then click on **Edit Text**.

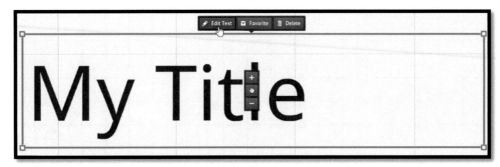

If you want to change a text item position, click and hold on the **Hand Tool** icon.

And you can increase or decrease the size of a text by using the (**+**) and (**-**) icons.

Finally if you want to delete a text item, just select that item and hit **Delete**.

Inserting and Editing Images

Use the **Insert** menu at the top to insert an image.

On the right hand side you are going to see an **Insert image** window. You can select a file from your computer by clicking on **Select files**...

After selecting the image file from your computer, click on **Open**.

Then the image will be simply added to your canvas.

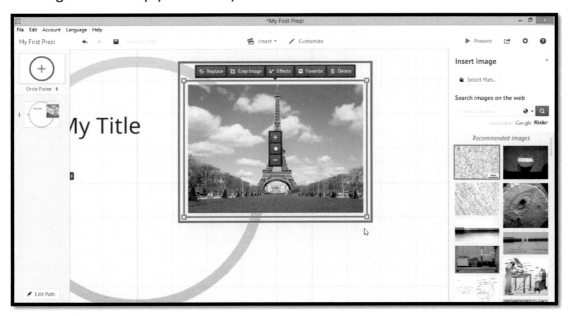

Or you can search for images from the web.

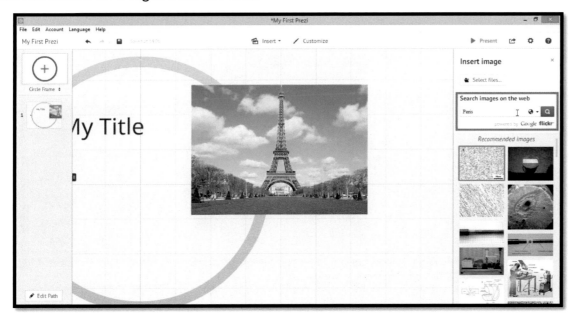

If you are searching for images for commercial use, just make sure to check this option:

This way Prezi will load images licensed for commercial use only, and the results of the web search will appear on the left of the screen under the search bar.

To insert an image from the web, double-click on it or click, hold and bring it to the canvas.

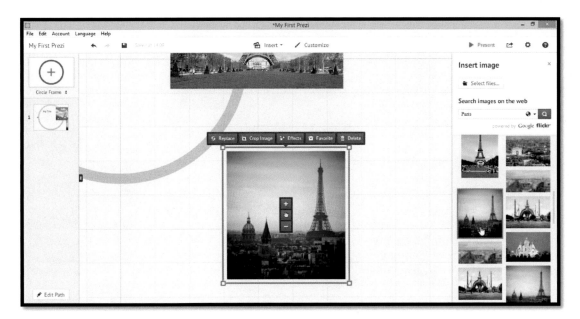

Once the images are part of your prezi, you can change their size by clicking and holding on the image corner then move the cursor a little further.

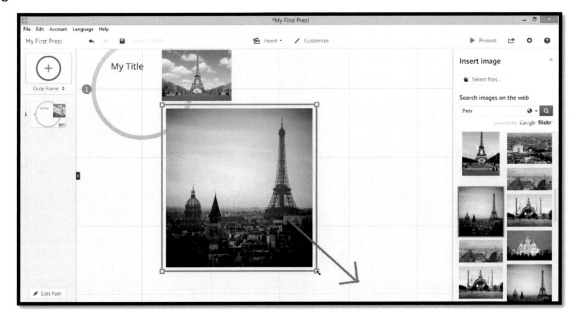

You can move them around by clicking and holding the **Hand Tool**.

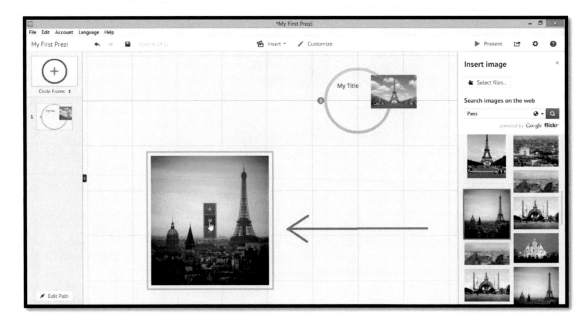

Or rotate them by clicking and holding the image corner.

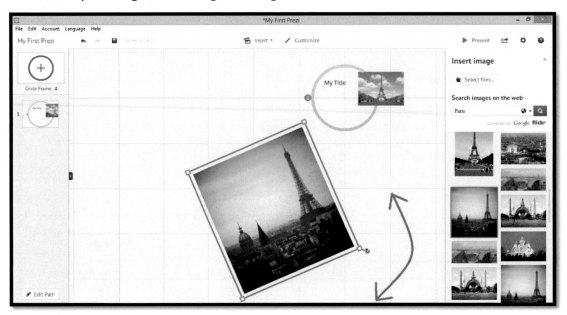

You can replace an image by another from your computer or from the web.

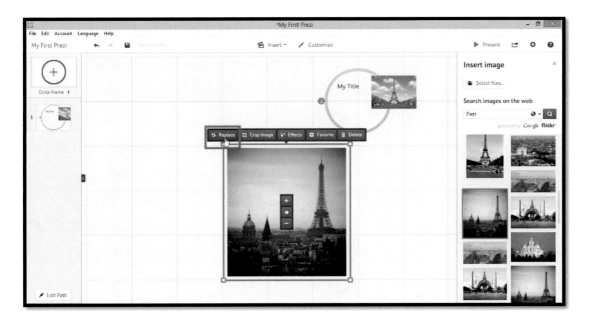

Or you can crop it.

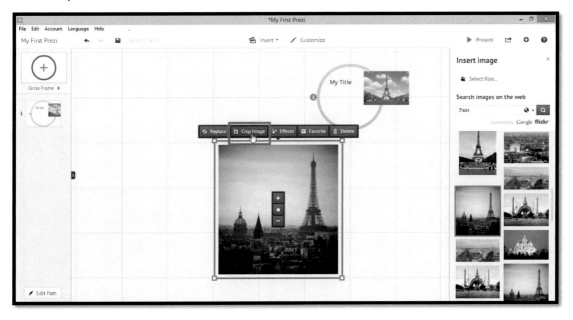

Just select the image zone that you want to keep.

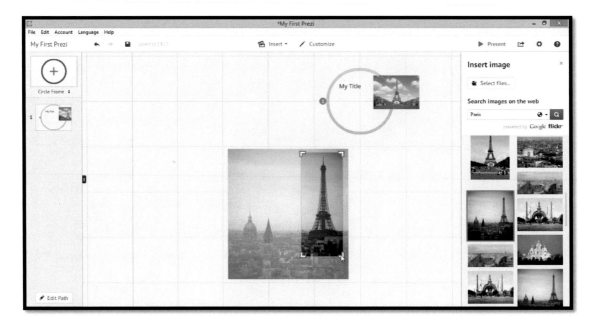

Then click **Enter** to crop.

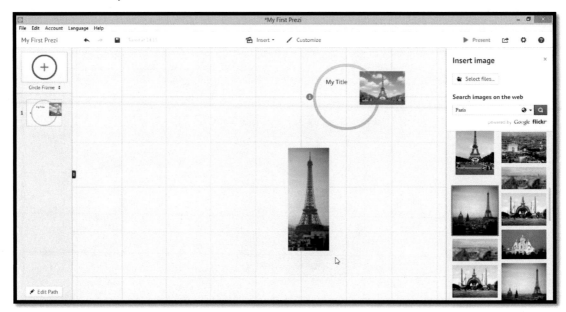

You may click on **Effects** for more editing options.

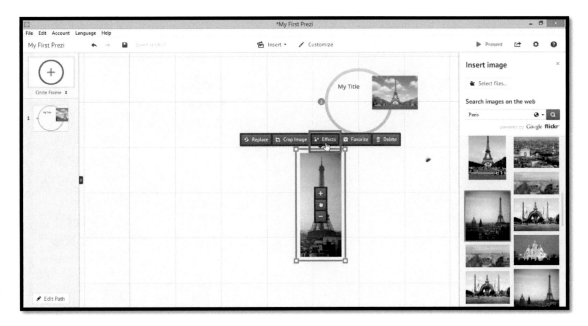

A new window will open with a list of effects such as Enhace, Warmth, Brightness..., Click on **Save** after finishing your modifications.

You can add an image to your list of favorites in order to re-use it later.

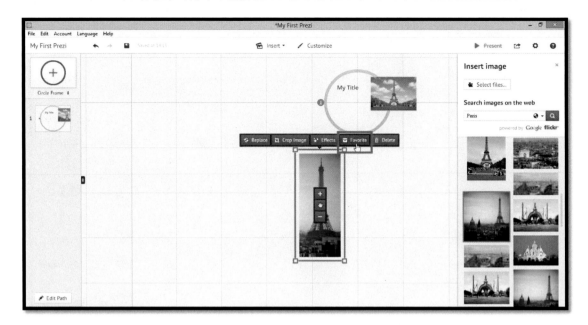

And you can delete an image.

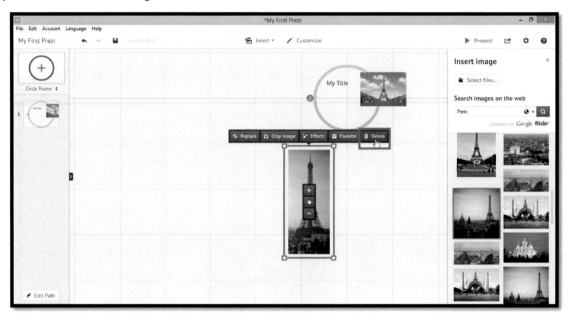

Objects in Prezi are layered on top of each other. When they are overlaid, the objects on top will display in front of the others.

30

You can change the order of objects by right-clicking on them; just find the appropriate order that you want such as **Bring Forward**, **Bring to Top**, **Send Backward**, and **Send to Back**.

Notice that the image that was in the back is now in front of the second.

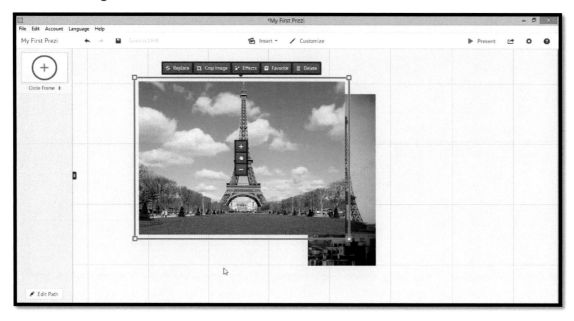

Lesson 3

Working with Frames & Paths in Prezi

It is now time to add new frames (slides) to your prezi. To add a frame, use the add button located at the top left of the screen.

And you can select what type of frame you want to add to your prezi, whether it is a circle, a bracket, a rectangle or an invisible frame.

Moreover, if you want to change the type of a frame after inserting it, you can click on this frame, then click on the icon above this frame, then change it.

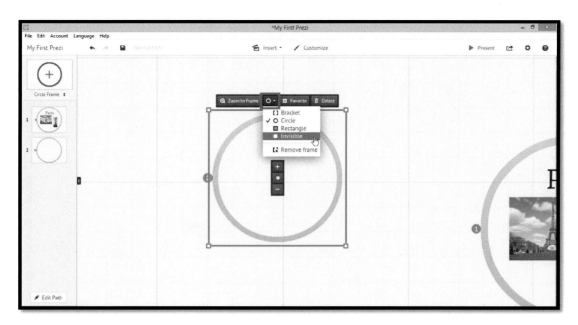

Another method to add frames is by clicking on the **Insert** button on the top of the screen, then click on **Layouts…**

And you can add a Single or Multi-Frame as explained before. To add the frame that you like, either double-click on it or click and drag it to the canvas.

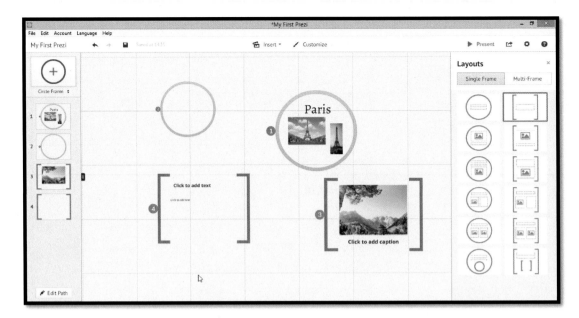

When you click on a frame on the left of the screen, Prezi will zoom it on the canvas.

The frames will keep the same order that you have inserted them in. You can change this order by clicking on **Edit Path**.

Currently, we have four frames in the path steps of our prezi. We can change the order of a frame in the path by clicking and holding on it, and then move it to its new position on the path.

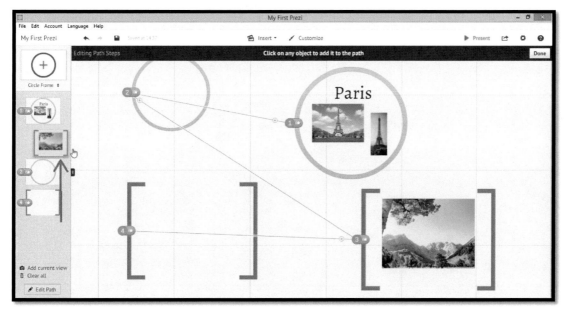

Or, you can edit path points by dragging numbers and dropping them.

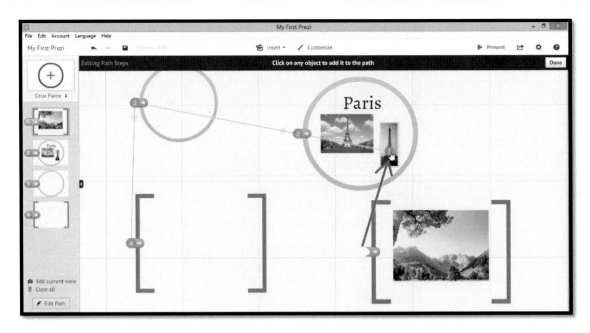

The little plus sign (**+**) on the path indicates that you can add additional path points to that line.

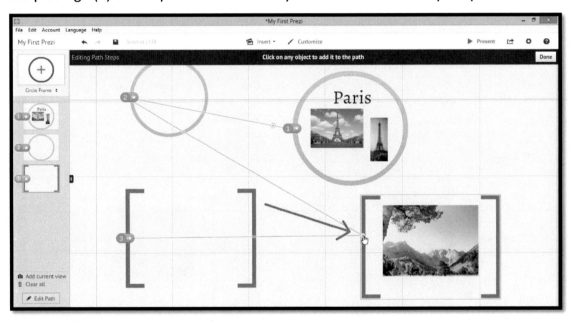

To remove a path point, you can click on **Edit Path** then click on the cross sign (**x**) on the path point that you want to delete.

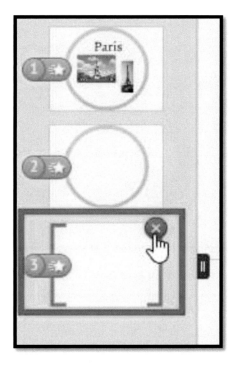

Or you can drag the path point number of this frame and drop it away on the canvas.

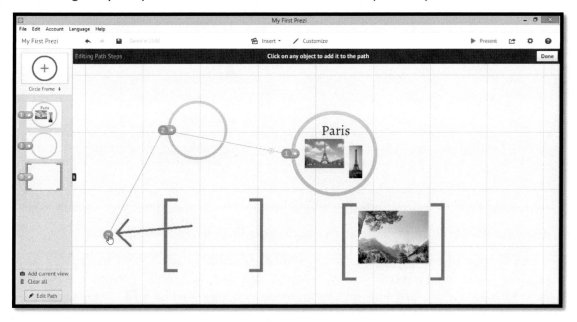

If you want to add an overview of the current frames, go ahead and click on **Add current view** at the lower left corner of your screen.

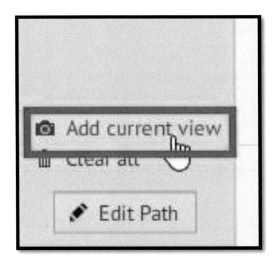

This will take a snapshot of your current view and add it as a new point to your path.

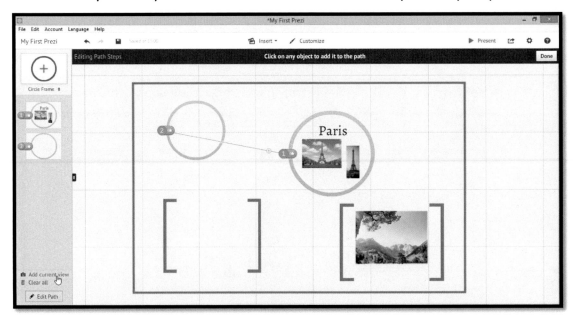

When you are done with editing your path, click on **Edit Path** to exit that mode.

To finalize this chapter, I should mention some notes regarding the frames in Prezi. You should know that when you insert items (texts, images...) inside a frame (circle, bracket...), they automatically become one object altogether. So when you change the size of the frame, you will change the size of the inside items as well.

You can increase the frame size by clicking and holding its corner exactly like an image.

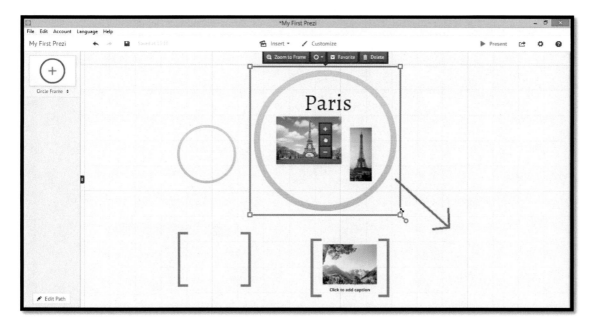

You can decrease its size as well with the same way.

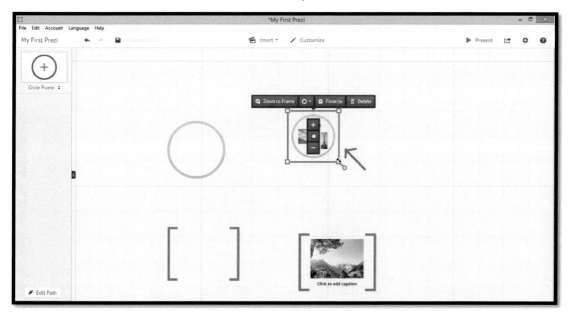

Moving frames is similar to moving other items. Just click and hold the **Hand Tool** to do so.

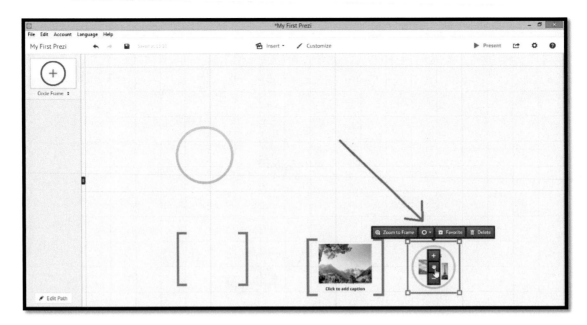

Another thing about frames. If you want to delete a frame but you want to keep its inside items, just right-click on it then click **Remove Frame without Deleting Content.**

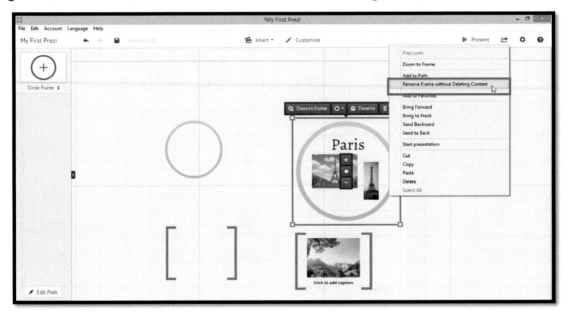

As you can see, the frame has gone but its content is always in the canvas.

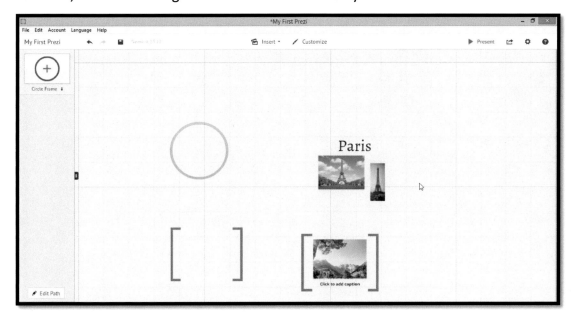

Lesson 4

Drawing Arrows and Lines
&
Adding Symbols, Shapes and Diagrams

Drawing Arrows

Drawing arrows and adding them to your prezi may help your audience to understand the flow of your presentation. Since Prezi's unique zooming approach may be difficult to adjust especially in the beginning, help your audience by visually guiding them so that they could see what is next with the help of arrows.

Let's add some arrows.

For example, I will draw one arrow between every two frames. (Notice that I have created four different frames, each one with a title and images in it, something you should be able to do at this stage).

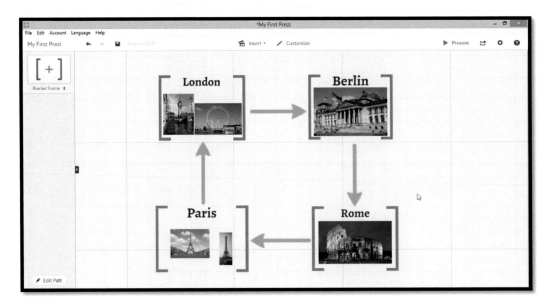

Notice that after you draw an arrow, you will be able to change its thickness, its color; add it to your favorites or delete it.

Another thing about arrows is that you can curve them by using the central path point.

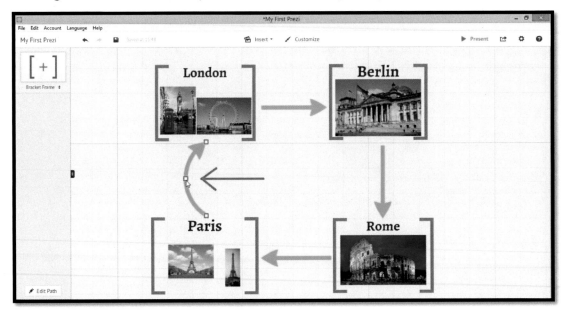

Drawing Lines

You can also add lines to your prezi.

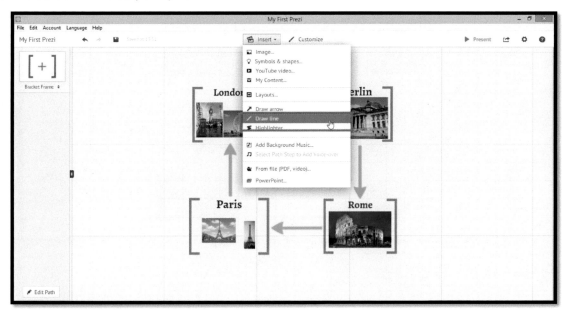

And change their style and thikness...

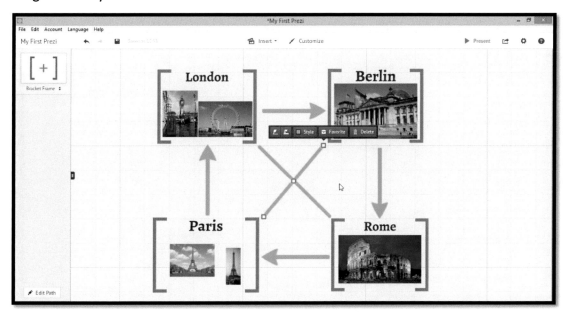

Lines can also be curved by using the central path point.

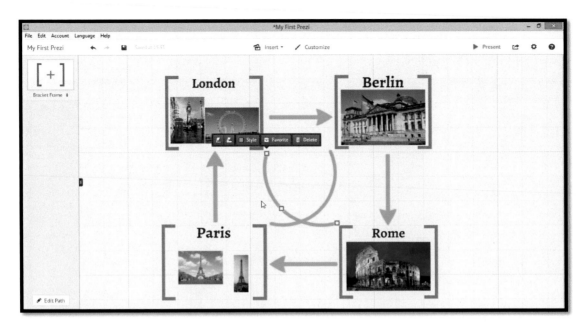

Adding Symbols & Shapes

You can add symbols and shapes to your Prezi presentation, they are similar to clip-arts in PowerPoint.

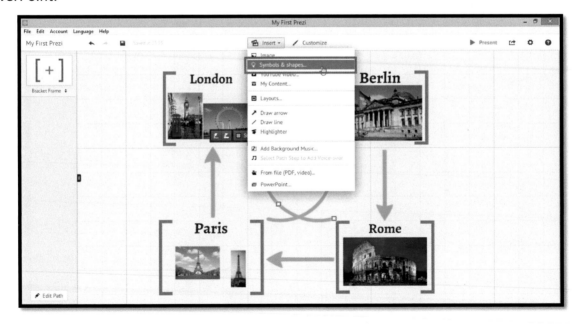

You can add different styles of symbols & shapes, such as Simple Dark, Simple White, Photographic...

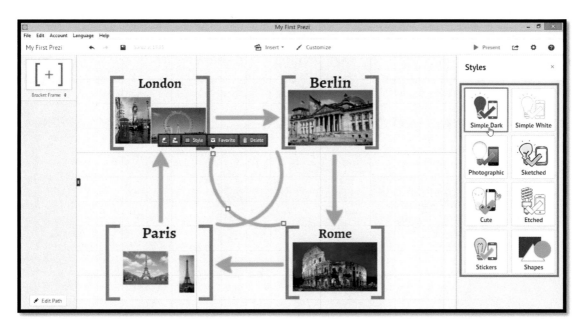

Just double-click on a symbol to add it to your presentation (or you can simply drag and drop it). In this example I am going to add a small airplane in the center of my frames.

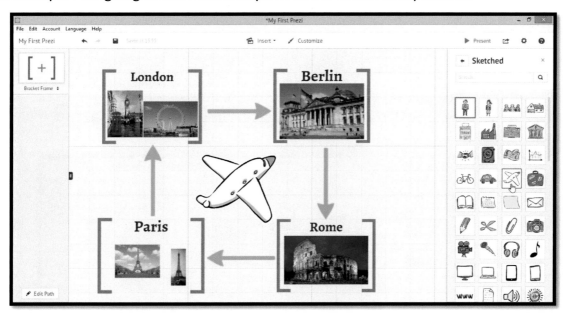

You can always change the size and rotate the clip-art using the transformation tool (just like the images and other items).

Adding Shapes

Shapes are located at the bottom, and they include basic shapes such as circles, rectangles and triangles. And you can add them either by double-clicking or dragging and dropping them in the canvas.

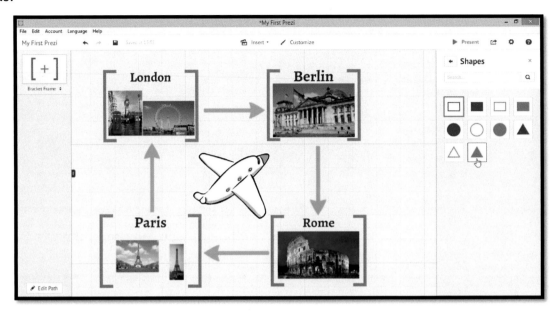

Adding Diagrams

Diagrams can be helpful when you want to show the relationship between objects. They are named in Prezi as Multi-Frames. To find them, click on the **Insert** menu, then **Layouts**, then **Multi-Frames**.

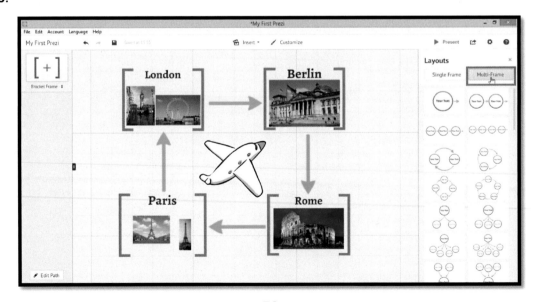

As you can see, there are different types of diagrams; such as: Linear, Cycle, Divergent, Convergent, Balance, Timeline, Iceberg… You can insert the most appropriate diagram for your presentation or you can modify it to meet your criteria.

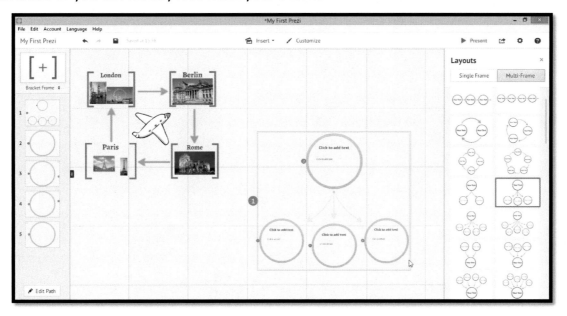

51

Lesson 5

*Adding Videos, Background Music
&
Voice-overs to Prezi*

Adding Video Files

You can add a video file from your computer. To do so, click on the **Insert** menu, then on **From file (PDF, video)...**

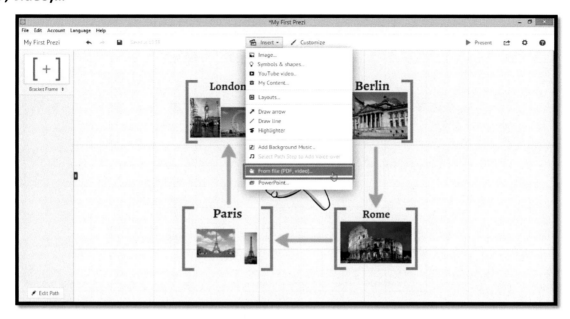

You can click on **Play** to check that your video is working.

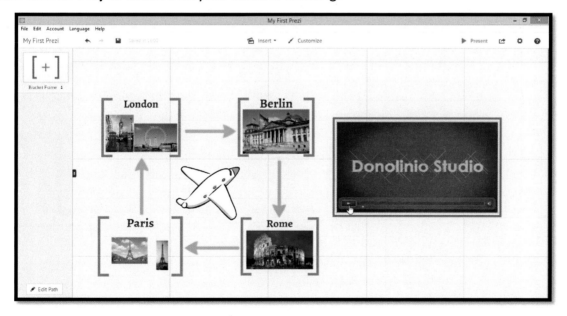

Remember that if you add the video to the path, it will be played automatically in the **Present** mode.

Adding YouTube Videos

To add a YouTube video to your presentation, just click **Insert** then select **YouTube video...**

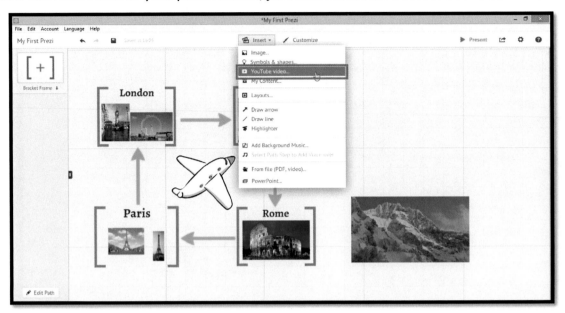

You will need to paste the link of your YouTube video, find the link of the video that you want to add, copy it then paste it in the window that will open. Then click on **Insert**.

As you can see, Prezi has added your YouTube video to the canvas. Remember that you can always rotate your video or rescale it using the transformation tool.

Adding Music Background

You may add background music to your presentation as well.

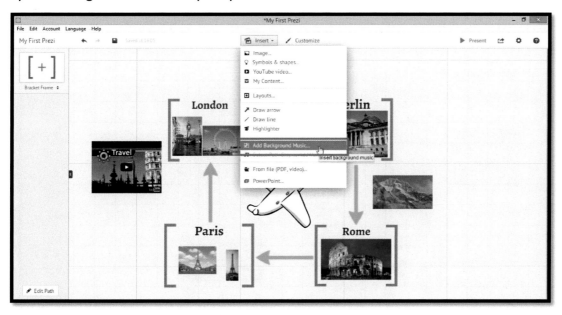

Simply click on **Add Background Music…** from the **Insert** menu, then choose the music file that you want to add from your computer. When the music file is uploaded, you will see that it is placed over your frames or path steps meaning that it will be played during your presentation in the background. You can click on **Play** to listen or preview your background music and you can always delete the background music by using the **Trash** icon.

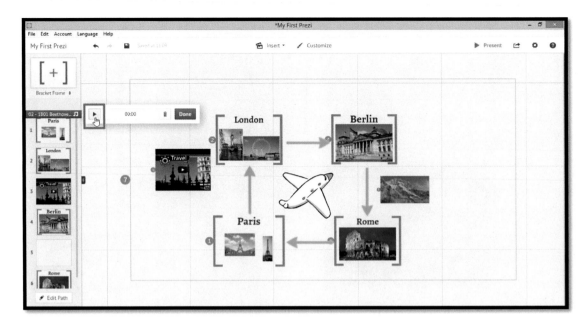

The music background will be played automatically when you start the **Present** mode, but you can always disable it using the **Mute** icon at the left bottom of the screen once you are in the **Present** mode.

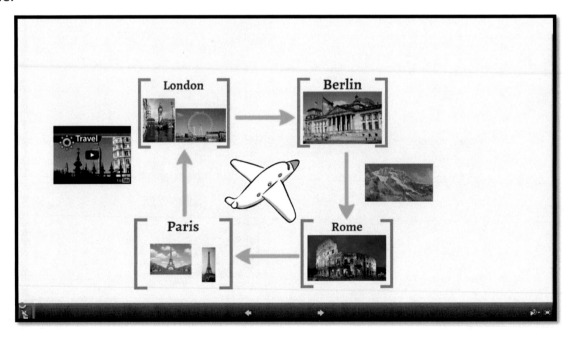

Adding Narrations

You can also narrate your frames or path steps. In order to add voice over, make sure you will be in the **Edit Path** mode.

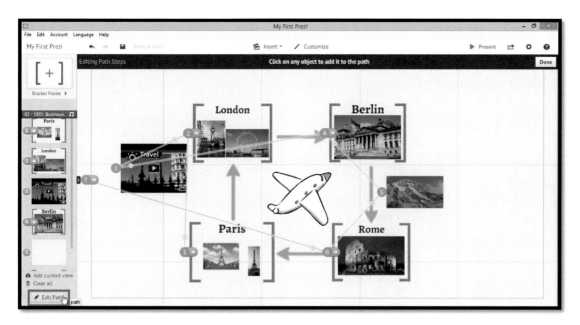

Select the frame that you want to narrate.

Then click on **Add Voice-over to Path Step #...**

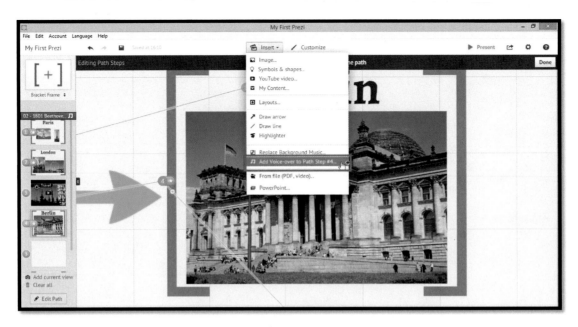

Make sure that you have already recorded the narration file then add it from your computer. Note that the narration file will be linked only to the frame that you added it to.

Again, the narration will be enabled only in the **Present** mode.

If you add both a background music and a narration, notice that the volume of the background music will be lowered automatically while playing the narration to allow to your narration to be heard during the presentation.

Lesson 6

Adding PowerPoint
&
PDF files to your prezi

Adding PowerPoint Slides

You may import PowerPoint and PDF files to your prezi. If you have your PowerPoint presentation already created, you can easily convert it to a prezi presentation. Prezi will allow you to do that with dedicated PowerPoint import tool under the **Insert** menu.

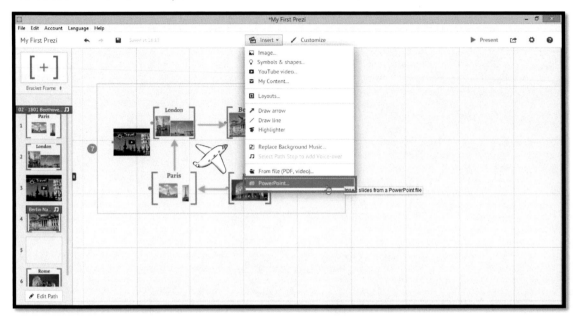

Prezi converts the PowerPoint slides into its own format, once the conversion is done, the uploaded slides will appear on the right of the screen under the **Import** tool.

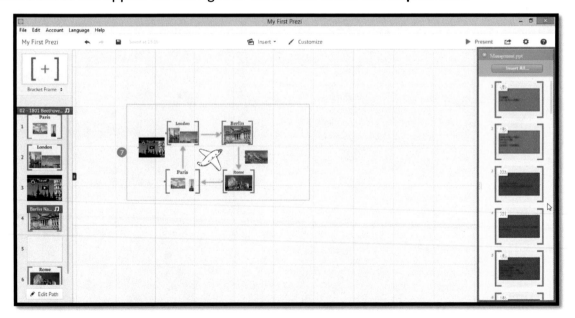

You can insert all slides by using **Insert All** at the top, or you can use **CTRL** or **Shift** key to insert only the slides that you need. You will also have the ability to insert them in a specific layout of your choice and add a path between them or not.

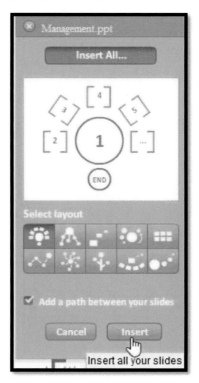

Drag the slides to your presentation and place them anywhere you like and click the check mark when finished.

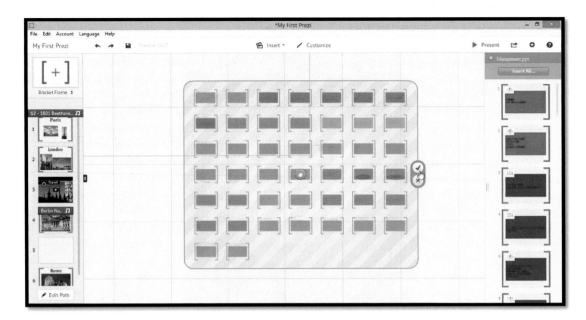

Adding PDF Files

You can also add PDF files to your prezi.

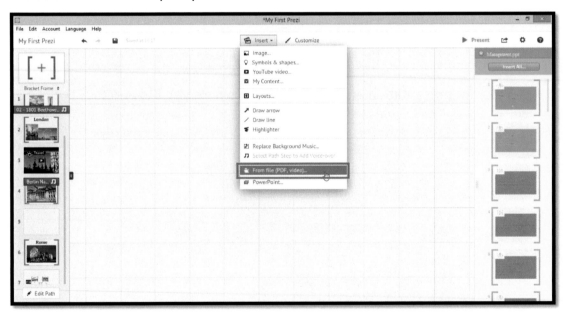

If your PDF file contains several pages, then Prezi will consider every single page as an image.

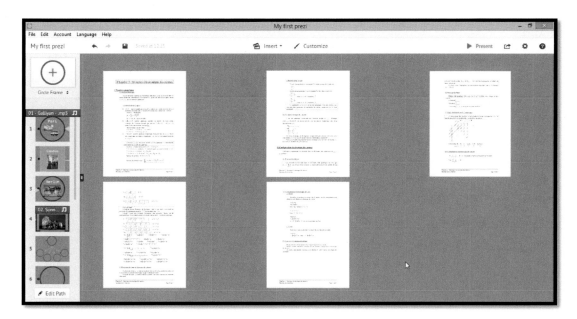

And you can apply all the operations related to images on these PDF pages, such as resizing, rotating and cropping...

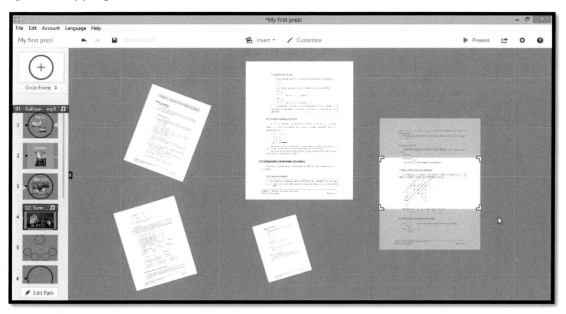

As you can see I have changed the prezi background from light grey to darker grey, in order to allow to the white PDF pages to appear more clearly.

Changing and customizing Prezi's background and themes will be our next topic.

Lesson 7

Customizing Themes
&
Creating prezis from Templates

Customizing Themes

In order to customize the current theme, click on the **Customize** icon at the top of the screen.

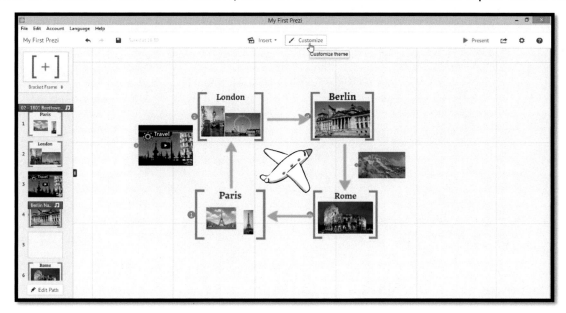

A **Customize** tool will open at the right of your screen.

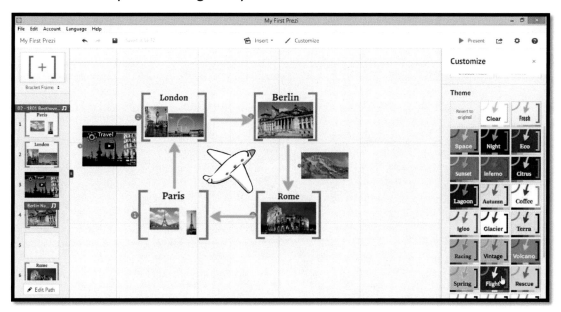

Choose a style you like.

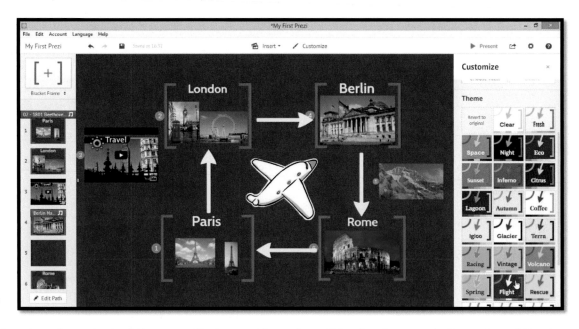

Notice that the selected theme will change the color of the background, the color of the texts, the color of the arrows, the color of the frames (circles, brackets...). Also it changes the font style of the texts. Let's say you like these changes except for the color of the background, click on **Advanced** to change it.

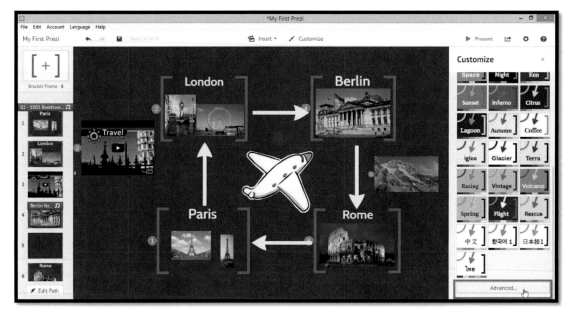

We're going to use the **Wizard** option first.

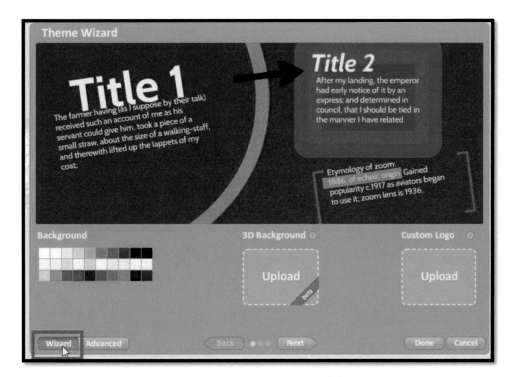

You can change the background color and see a preview in this window.

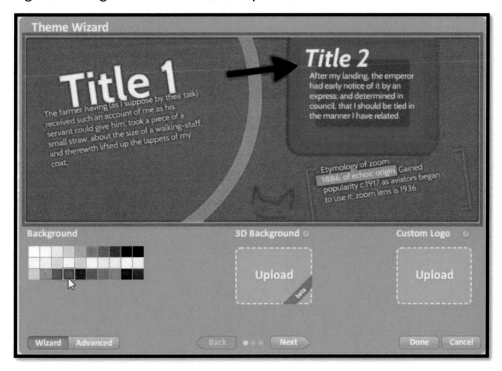

Then click **Next** to adjust Fonts and Colors. Here you can change the font and the color of your Title 1, Title 2 and the Body text.

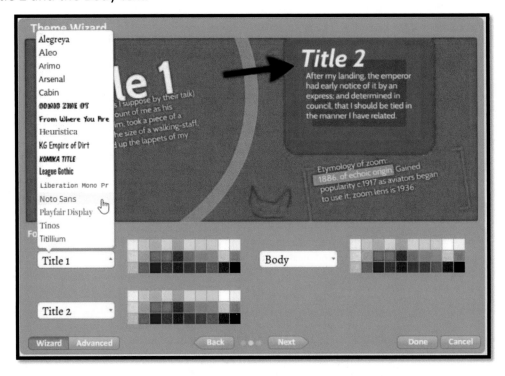

Click **Next** to adjust shapes. Here you can change the colors of your frames, the colors of your arrows and lines, and also the color with which you want to highlight your texts.

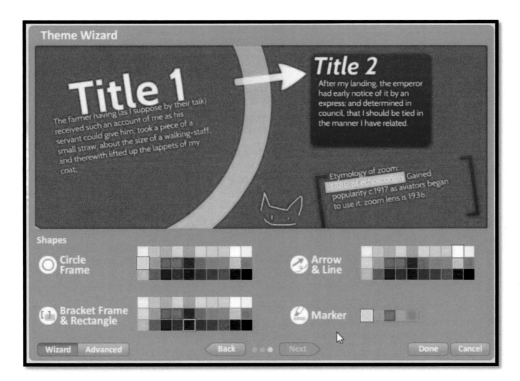

Click **Done** when you finish.

Here is our new customized theme.

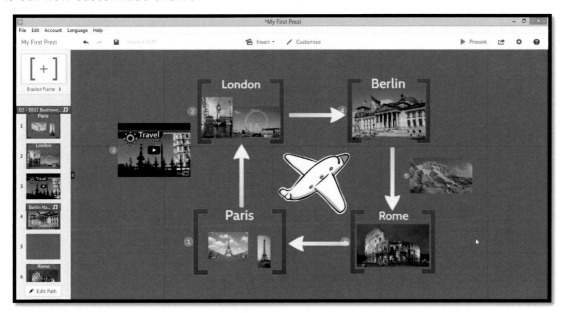

If you like these changes you can actually keep them. Click on **Customize**, then on **Save current theme**.

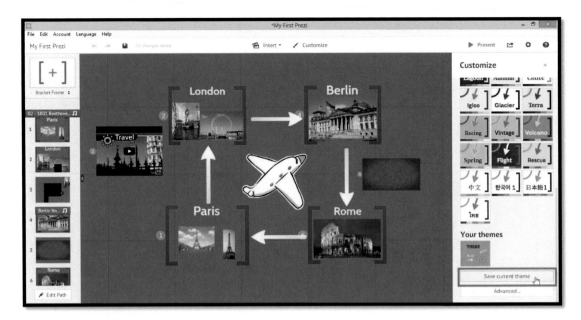

Your new customized theme will be saved and it will appear under **Your themes**.

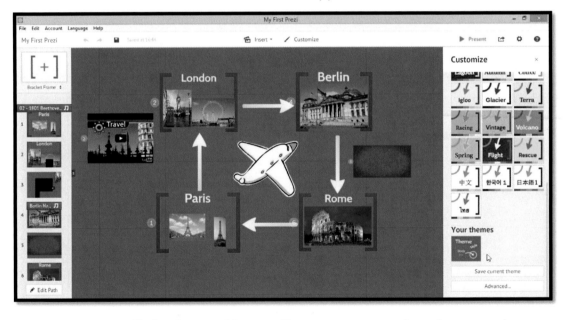

If you want to use a specific background image, like your company logo for example, you can add it as well. Just click on **Choose file** in the **Customize** tool.

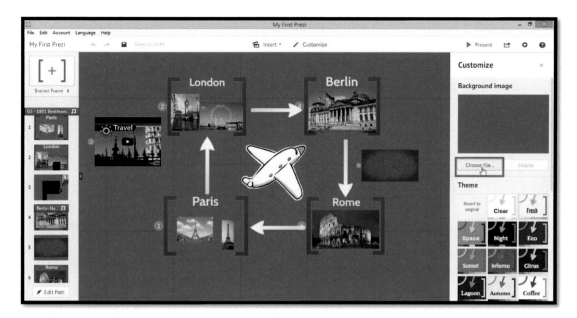

Select the image that you want to use as a background from your computer.

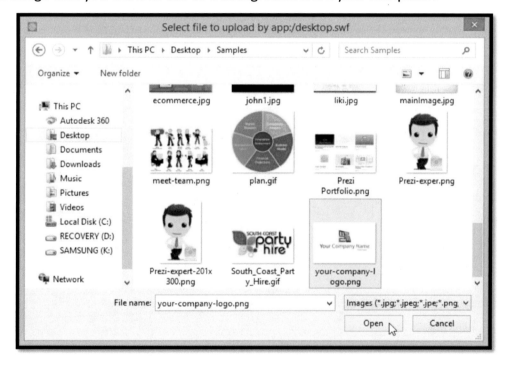

Then click on **Open**.

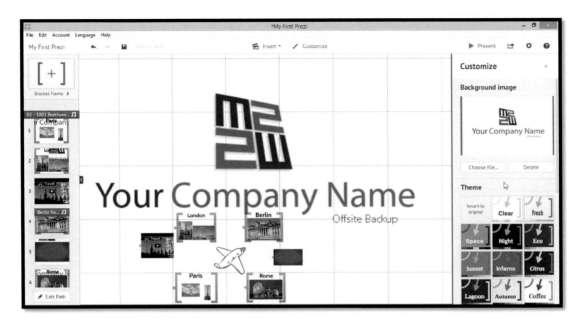

Adding Custom Logo

In Prezi you can also add a custom logo that will appear during all the presentation in the bottom left corner of the screen (in **Present** mode only). To do so, click on **Advanced** in the **Customize** tool, make sure you are in the **Wizard** mode, click on **Upload** below **Custom Logo** and upload your logo file from your computer.

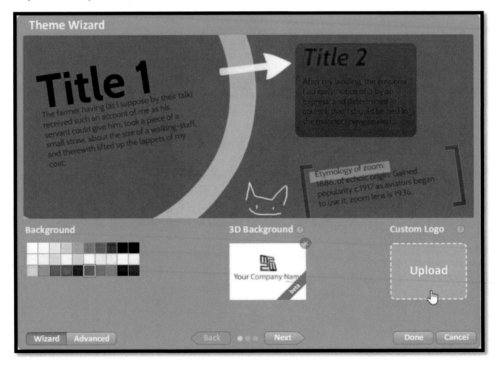

As you can see in the image below, the logo will appear in the bottom left of the screen during all the presentation.

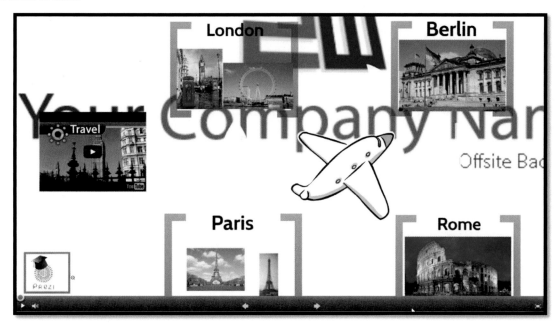

Creating Presentations from Templates

Next, we are going to create a presentation from a template in Prezi. Click on **New Prezi** icon on your Prezi home page, but this time, instead of starting blank presentation, select **Use template**. You will see a list of templates, as well as a list of **Popular Templates**. These are built-in templates that you can use freely and modify them as you need. You can also search for templates if you like, just tape a keyword to search for a template.

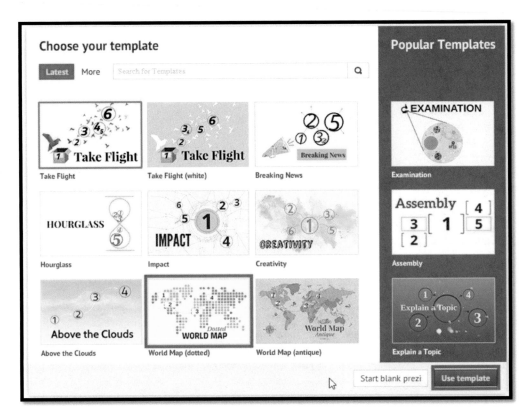

I will select World Map template (to use a template, click on it then click **Use template**).

Notice that the path steps of any template you will use are already set in place.

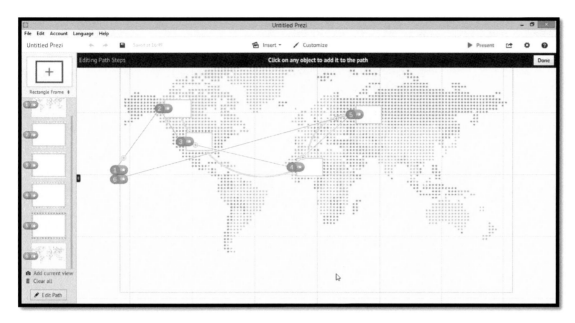

So you can keep these path steps and put your content in this template, taking into consideration the path steps, or you can edit the path using the **Edit Path** icon, in order to become more relevant to your content and your presentation.

Templates are a great addition to your Prezi presentations. And they will allow you to prepare creative presentations, or give you some ideas on what to do for your presentation. If you are in a hurry and you do not want to worry about path points, just use templates.

Lesson 8

Sharing & Collaboration in Prezi

Sharing in Prezi

You can share your Prezi presentations with your friends, colleagues or clients... To do so, your prezi have to be synced with Prezi.com website. Click on **Sync with Prezi.com** if it is not synced yet.

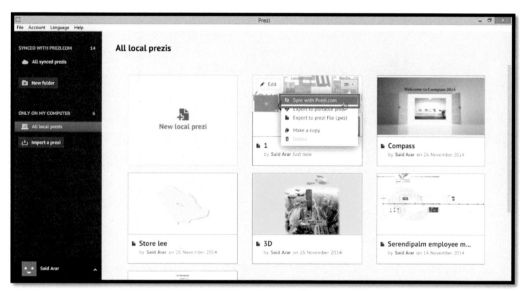

Then enter to your Prezi.com profile and click on **Share** for the presentation that you want to share.

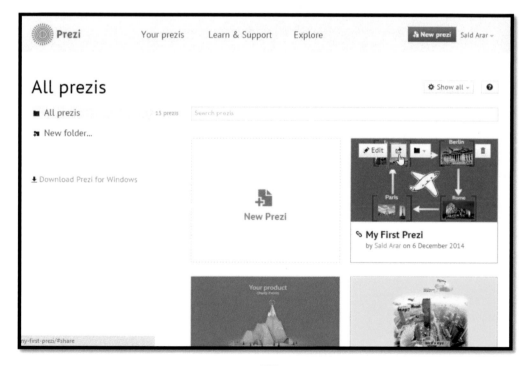

The following window will open.

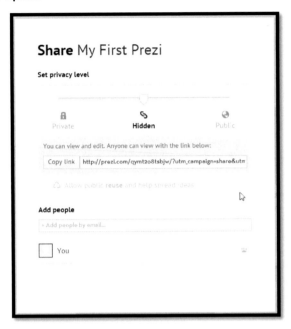

As you can see, you can keep this presentation only for yourself by clicking on **Private**. You can share it with only the people that you want, by selecting **Hidden** then giving them the link; or you can just make this presentation **Public** if this is what you want. You can also share the presentation with anyone by adding their email below, and you can make this person even only a **Viewer** of this presentation or an **Editor** as well.

Remember that these Privacy & Sharing options are for Prezi paid licenses only such as **Enjoy** and **Pro**…, if you have a free **Public** license, all your prezis will be public.

Collaboration in Prezi

Remote presentation allows anyone with your presentation link to follow your presentation live without the need to signing up or login to Prezi.com. You can start this feature by clicking on **Present remotely**.

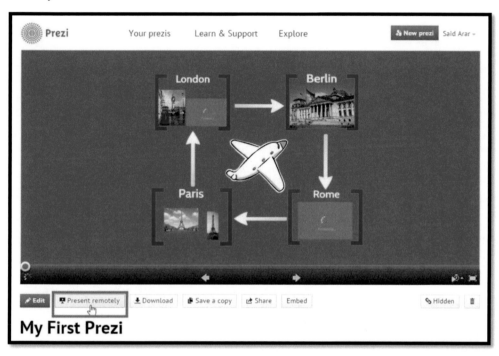

Then copy the link of the presentation and send it to your audience.

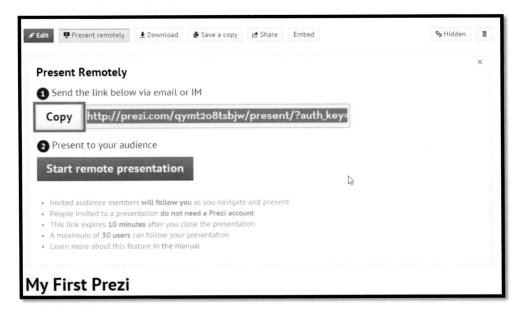

When you want to start the remote presentation, just click on **Start remote presentation**. Let's say that the browser on the left is my browser while I am presenting, and the browser on the right is the browser of one of my audience after he opened the link that I sent to him.

As you can see, I can start presenting and my audience will be able to follow my presentation at the same time with me. Notice that you still can open the **Edit** mode and edit your presentation, but your audience will only have the prezi on **Present** mode.

Lesson 9

Advanced Techniques in Prezi

Adding 3D Backgrounds to Prezi

In order to add 3D backgrounds to your presentation, you need to click on **Customize**, then on **Customize current theme** (make sure you are in **Advanced** mode), and click **Edit** for 3D Background.

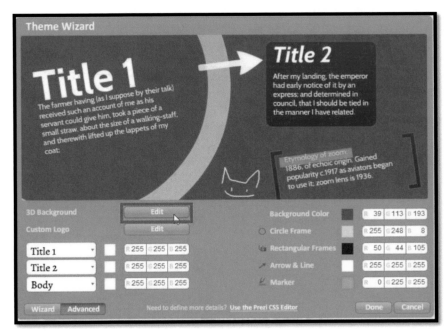

You can upload up to 3 images, please make sure that the images are in HD resolution (3000 pixels wide).

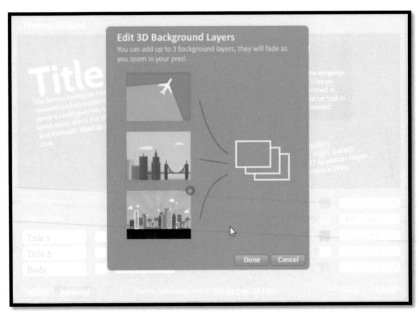

Click **Done** when you have finished. What is going to happen when you insert these images, is that they will be layered on top of each other as a background images; your first image at the top will also be at the top of the other images in the same order.

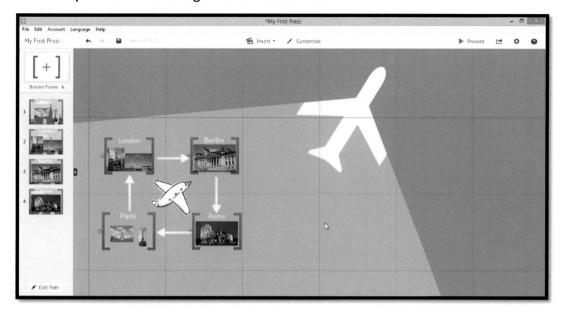

When you will zoom in enough in the canvas, the image at the top will fade out, and the image down will fade in, and when you further zoom in, you will be able to see your third image layered at the bottom – That is a 3D effect.

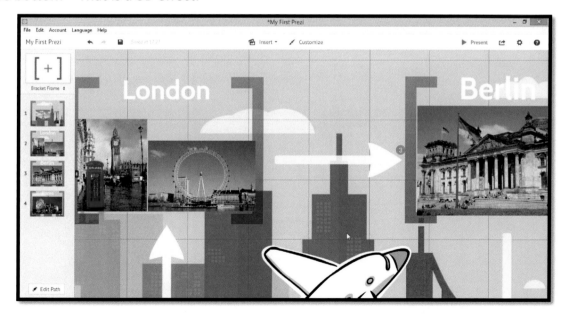

Inserting Hyperlinks to Prezi

Select a location where you want to add your hyperlink. You can copy the link from your browser or tape it yourself just like you are taping a text. Just make sure to start with **http://** otherwise your link will not be recognized by Prezi. To check that your link works, just click away to see if it is underlined. If it is, this means that Prezi has recognized the link.

If you want to open your hyperlink on a new browser window, you will have to be in **Present** mode.

Animating Frame Content

In Prezi you can animate the content of your frames. In order to do this, make sure you click on **Edit Path** mode first.

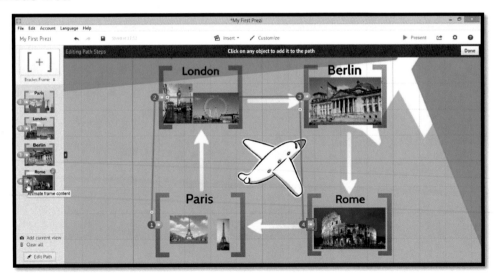

Next to the path step number of the frame that you want to edit, you are going to see a star symbol (★).Click on that star to animate the contents. You will have a window similar to this one.

Click on the objects where you would like to apply the animation effect. Currently there is only one animation effect in Prezi which is the classic **Fade-in** effect. You can add the animation effect to all the objects inside the frame; the animation effect will be inserted in the order of your application. You will see numbers next to objects, which means that the animation will be played in this specific order.

You can click on the animation number to remove the effect.

You can preview the animation by clicking on **Play**.

If you want all the objects to fade in at the same time, use the **Grouping** option. Click on the objects that you want to group together while holding **Shift** or **CTRL** then click on **Group**.

Then you can redo the animation operation.

Saving Your Work

Prezi saves your work continuously on the computer where you are working and uploads it to your Prezi.com account. But if you want to take your work and open it in another computer, you will be able to do this by exporting your presentation as a Prezi file (**.pez**).

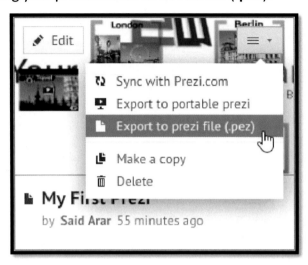

This option allows you to present or edit your work using another computer. Just keep in mind that you will need Prezi to be installed in order to open the (**.pez**) file.

Another option to take your work with you is to save it as an **Exportable Prezi File**. This option does not require having the Prezi software installed in the computer that you want to use. But you will only be able to present without the ability to edit.

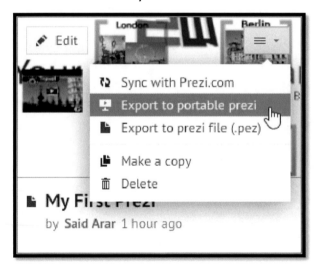

Lesson 10

10 Tips To Design Great Prezis

1. Start by mind-mapping your presentation, keep in mind the fact that people will not likely remember more than five sections from your overview. Start creating sections and put all the pieces you want in those sections. Prezi templates are a good example on how to organize your content.

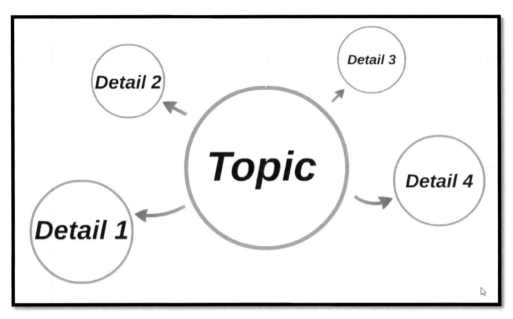

2. Create a meaningful structure. The best prezis are those that have a meaningful structure to them, so in the completely zoomed out view, your audience sees what your whole presentation is about, like a map or floorplan.

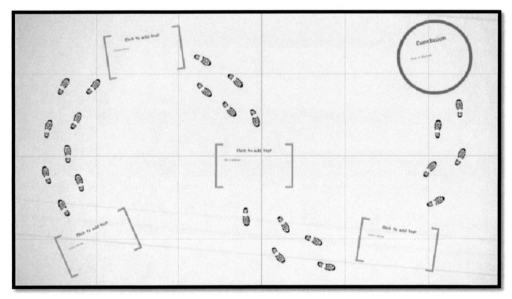

3. While you can have many levels of zooming, the best presentations have only three layers of depth in zooming, so your audience does not get lost in the forest as they walk through the trees.

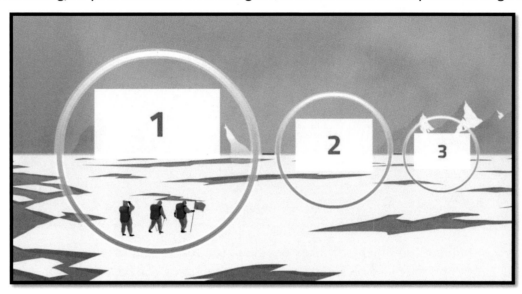

4. Images make very cool narrations and also trigger emotions. It's great to use a metaphorically relevant background image that can serve as a container for the entire presentation or just a section.

5. Show your context often. It is good to insert a slightly zoomed out interstitial frame once in a while to give the viewer some special context during the presentation. So they know where they are in the journey across the Prezi canvas.

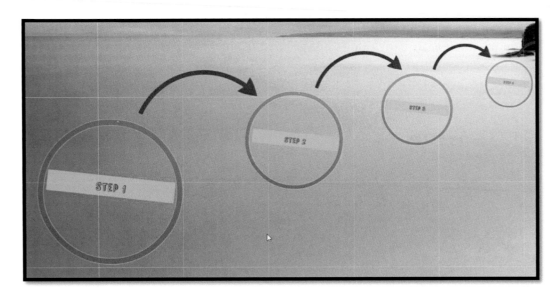

6. Refrain from spinning too much. It makes people nauseous and unless you are making a point about taking a new perspective, you should avoid dramatic spins. The best prezis rotate only a few degrees from object to object.

7. Use visual guides. Arrows or other visual objects help to guide the movement from one frame to another, so that the viewer does not get lost in space.